# THE RUINS OF THE HEART

# THE RUINS
# OF THE HEART

*Selected Lyric Poetry of*
# JELALUDDIN RUMI
*Translated by Edmund Helminski*

THRESHOLD BOOKS • PUTNEY

© 1981, Edmund Helminski, all rights reserved.
Third edition.

Cover illustration from the *Khamsa* of Nizami,
courtesy of the trustees of the British Museum.

ISBN 0-939660-03-2

Library of Congress Catalog Number: 83-145353

Book design by Edmund Helminski.

# Contents

Introduction

Lyric Poetry

Appendix: A Note on the Thirteenth Century.

*Dedicated to my wife and fellow-traveler, Camille.*

# Introduction

Western culture has no convenient category for Mevlána Jeláluddín Rúmí. In the Islamic world he is held in the highest esteem not only as a literary figure, but as a saint whose personal example inspired the founding of a major religious order, and as a philosopher whose elaboration of the cosmic sense of Love has had a significant cultural impact.

His literary genius is made clear in the 30,000 verses of impassioned lyric poetry in his *Diván-i Shamsi Tabríz* and in the 22,000 verses of his masterwork, the *Mathnawí*, a vast tapestry into which has been woven Aesopian fables, scenes from the everyday life of his times, Koranic revelation, and Neoplatonic metaphysics. The great poet Abdur-Rahmán Jámí called the *Mathnawí* "the Koran in the Persian tongue." Sa'dí, another major poet, once selected an ode of Mevlána's for presentation to the Moghul Khan as the best poem in the Persian language. In the West Rúmí's influence has been felt by Chaucer, Goethe, and Emerson, to name a few; and no less a critic than Doctor Johnson has said of him: "He makes plain to the Pilgrim the secrets of the Way of Unity, and unveils the Mysteries of the Path of Eternal Truth."

To many already familiar with his life and writings, Mevlána Jeláluddín Rúmí is something more than a poet. He might be considered an example of *Insáni kámil*, perfected or completed man, a human being in whom the divine attributes are embodied. A figure of almost prophetic dimensions, he became for some Muslims almost a second Muhammed, for Christians a second Christ, and for Jews a second Moses. Among those present at his funeral procession were people of different religious traditions each of whom claimed that Jeláluddín had brought him to a deeper understanding of his own faith.

Rúmí's work can be considered a synthesis of all that Islamic culture had assimilated from Arab, Hellenistic, Hermetic, Christian, Jewish, Persian, and Indian sources in the first seven hundred years of its existence. With complete respect for the prophets of the Judaeo-Christian-Islamic tradition, and with uncommon beauty and insight, he elucidated the mythic inheritance, the shared traditions of his age; yet he was somehow beyond his own culture and time. Although following the details of the Islamic faith, Rúmí expounded a religion of Love. Without denying his own Islamic faith he was able to say, "The religion of Love is like no other," and "Gambling yourself away is beyond any religion."

For the Sufis, the gnostics of Islam, Love has always been a central theme. In Persia especially, the metaphor of Love, Lover, and Beloved was developed so vividly that its metaphoric significance was sometimes mistaken for wanton sensuality. The Andalusian philosopher-saint, Ibn 'Arabí, authored some of the most beautiful love poetry in the Arabic language at the same time that he developed one of the most comprehensive systems of metaphysics ever known. When compelled to defend his poetry against orthodox detractors, he was more than able to demonstrate that the language of love was an appropriate analog for spiritual realities. For Rúmí, especially, Love was the very cause of existence, the hand behind the puppets, the Grand Artificer.

When in middle age he met the vagabond alchemist, Shamsi Tabríz, Mevlána said, "The God which I have worshipped all my life appeared to me today in human form." This statement, however, should not be understood as the complete identification of the human and the divine. From the Islamic point of view no human being, not even the Prophet, could be identified with God. Nevertheless, for the Sufi mystic the phenomenal world is a bridge to the Real, and both Mevlána and Shams found in each other the most perfect example of the Friend. In each other's presence they were able to experience the unity of Love, Lover, and Beloved.

The meeting of Shams and Mevlána was like the conjunction of two great planets. They retired into a solitude which became legendary; but as in the conjunction of the sun and moon, the apparent darkness of eclipse was objectionable to some of Mevlána's former students. Jealousy arose and Shams departed suddenly, leaving Mevlána without the spiritual intimacy which they had enjoyed. Perhaps it was necessary that he experience the pain of separation in order to reach his own perfection. After some years Shams would return and meet his death at the hands of assassins, but not before Rúmí was completely transformed by his ardent love.

Mevlána would continue to discover the "Friend" in various guises through the rest of his life. After Shams it was Saláhuddín, a goldsmith who became a disciple, that Jelál would extol for his incomparable sanctity, and after Saláhuddín's death, Husámuddín, the recorder of the *Mathnawí*. Characteristic of Rúmí's spirituality is the recognition of the Beloved or Friend in human form, not as the worship of personality, but as a recognition of the spiritual gifts the One continually bestows on His creatures. For Rúmí, as for many who have followed his way through the centuries, friendship and love are essential values. In the *Menáqibu l'Arifín* Ahmed El Afláki, disciple of the grandson of Rúmí, relates the following story on the subject of humility and respect:

*Jelál spoke a parable from the trees of the field: "Every tree that yields no fruit, as the pine, the cypress, the*

11

*box, etc., grows tall and straight, lifting its head up high, and sending all its branches upward; whereas all the fruit bearing trees droop their heads, and trail their branches."* ... *In like manner, Jelál also had the commendable habit to show himself humble and considerate to all, even the lowest; especially so to children and old women. He used to bless them, and always bowed to them, even though these were not Muslims. Once he chanced upon a number of children who were playing, and who left their game, ran to him, and bowed. Jelál bowed to them also; so much so, that one little fellow called out from afar: "Wait for me until I come." Jelál did not move away, until the child had come, bowed, and been bowed to.*

*At that time people were speaking and writing against him. Legal opinions were obtained and circulated, to the effect that music, singing and dancing, are unlawful. Out of his kindly disposition and love of peace, Jelál made no reply: and after a while all his detractors were silenced, and their writings clean forgotten, as though they had never been written; whereas, his family and followers will endure to the end of time, and will go on increasing continually.*

The subject of Rúmí's poetry is not life, but something altogether more than life. While most poetry leads us through carefully arranged thoughts and feelings, Rúmí writes from somewhere beyond thought and feeling as we know it: "Your thoughts are the bar behind the door! Set the wood on fire! Silence, heart!" His poetry is not so much the search for some immanent truth and knowledge, some discovery to be made in the outer world, but an elaboration of an instant *hereness*, the immediate inner song of experience that floods this world but is not of it. It is an ecstasy of knowledge that overflows into words, sounds, images.

His is a knowledge of the Whole as well as the parts.

Rúmí is building a model of an immense inner world using every possible example and situation of the outer world as metaphor. The spiritual and poetic tradition that produced Rúmí, Saná'í, 'Attár, Sa'di and Jámi, understands all of creation as providing the metaphors of Divine Qualities. Rúmí says that after seeing the face of one's Lord, the "whole earthly realm is fraud and fantasy." The Beloved, even when encountered in physical form, is just the exemplification of a spiritual Beloved entirely beyond form. If he mentions idols, he does not mean the literal idols of precious metals, but the idols that are inwardly held, the representations of Reality that usurp the place of immediate perception. If he speaks of intoxication, he means the spiritual states which are a kind of sobriety compared to the intoxication of conventional life. Very little is what it appears to be. The Sufi poet inhabits many worlds simultaneously, "worlds within worlds," and therefore it is possible to speak of each line having at least seven levels of meaning, each corresponding to one of the seven heavens or worlds of Islamic cosmology.

While some poetry may attempt to break conventions of language and style, this poetry does more than that. It attempts to disturb conventions of thought and feeling, to peel back the skin of conditioning, to penetrate layers of expectation. Especially in the *Mathnawí*, his method is to build on a theme with stories, images, ideas, diversions, approaching the center from all points on the periphery, intending to elucidate what can only be called "the mysteries." Whether it is the melody of spiritual separation and solitude, or the experience of connectedness and unity, it is sung with passion and immediacy. It is not an immediacy entirely absent from Western literatures, but this refinement of feeling is seldom found so unalloyed, so undiluted.

Rúmí's work is not the product of literary ambition,

but an act of service. Most of his lyric poetry was spoken spontaneously and recorded by its hearers. Rumí did not make too much of his own poetry. He once said that just as a host must plunge his hands into the cleaning of tripe, because that is what his guest has an appetite for, so he occupied himself with poetry. Afláki, however, relates these words of Mevlána's concerning his verses:

> *The great Causer of all causes caused a source of affection to arise, and out of the wilderness of causelessness raised a means by which I was attracted from the land of Khorasán to the land of the Romans (Asia Minor). That country he made a home for my children and posterity, in order that, with the elixir of grace, the copper of their existences might be transmuted into gold and into philosopher-stone, they themselves being received into the communion of saints. When I perceived that they had no inclination for the practice of religious austerities, and no knowledge of the divine mysteries, I imagined to arrange metrical exhortations and musical services, as being captivating for men's minds, and especially so for the Romans, who are naturally of a lively disposition and fond of incisive expositions. Even as a sick child is coaxed into taking a salutary, though nauseous medicine, in like manner, were the Romans led by art to acquire a taste for spiritual truth.*

Although Rúmí was one of the first of the major Persian poets to receive the attention of the West and numerous translations have been completed, it has been about seventy years since the publication of the English translations on which we depend. With all respect for James Redhouse, the great R.A.Nicholson, and his student, A.J.Arberry, what we have so far in English are accurate word for word versions in Victorian prose. Even Arberry, the most recent of the three has confessed: "These versions, being in the vast majority the first renderings into a Western language, and intended primarily for non-specialists, have been made as literal as possible, with a minimum concession to readability."

From the beginning my intention has been to present accurate translations of the texts as poetry in contemporary English. Although I did not wish to duplicate the meter and rhyme of the original, I have made an effort to remain true to its tone, and to find a rhthym consonant with its meaning.

The problem of translating Rúmí has two aspects that I would like to mention. First, the translator must not only acquaint himself with the cultural background of the work, but should have some affinity or experience with the esoteric traditions out of which the poetry grew. Secondly, he must find or create equivalent terms for experiences that might themselves be almost anachronistic to the modern mentality. I agree with the poet and critic Kathleen Raine who has said that the work of any serious artist or poet in our time is "to recreate a common language for the communication of knowledge of spiritual realities, and of the invisible order of the psyche."

I present these modest translations as a necessary if faltering step in that direction. I wish to thank the people who have encouraged this work, and especially Marzieh Gail who has guided my study of the Persian language, led me line by line through the beauty of Mevlána's work, and without whom I could not have attempted these translations. I would also like to express my deep gratitude to Shaikh Suleyman Hayati Dede of the Mevlevi Order, successor to Mevlána Jeláluddín Rúmí, whose kind example and understanding brought me closer to a living experience and taste of the essence of Mevlána's life.

*Edmund Helminski*

*I* am a sculptor, a molder of form.
In every moment I shape an idol.
But then, in front of you, I melt them down.
I can rouse a hundred forms and mix them with spirit,
but when I look into your face,
I want to throw them in the fire.
Do you merely fill this drunkard's glass?
Or do you really oppose the sober?
Is it you who brings to ruin every house I build?
My soul spills into yours and is blended.
Because my soul has absorbed your fragrance, I cherish it.
Every drop of blood I spill says to the earth:
I blend with my Beloved when I participate in love.
In this house of mud and water
my heart has fallen into ruins.
Enter this house, my Love, or let me leave.

*L*ove is reckless; not reason.
Reason seeks a profit.
Love comes on strong, consuming herself, unabashed.

Yet in the midst of suffering
Love proceeds like a millstone,
hard surfaced and straight-forward.

Having died to self-interest,
she risks everything and asks for nothing.
Love gambles away every gift God bestows.

Without cause God gave us Being;
without cause give it back again.
Gambling yourself away is beyond any religion.

Religion seeks grace and favor,
but those who gamble these away are God's favorites,
for they neither put God to the test nor knock at the
        door of gain and loss.

Mathnawí,VI, 1967-1974.

*L*isten to the reed and the tale it tells,
  how it sings of separation:
ever since they cut me from the reed bed,
my wail has caused men and women to weep.
I want a breast torn and tattered with longing,
so that I may relate the pain of love.
Whoever has been parted from his source
wants back the time of being united.
At every gathering I play my lament.
I've become a companion of happy and sad.
Each befriended me from his own ideas,
and none searched out the secrets within me.
My secret is not different from my lament,
but the senses cannot perceive it.
The body is not hidden from the soul,
nor the soul from the body, but the sight
of the soul is not for everyone.
This flute is played with fire, not with wind;
and without this fire you would not exist.
It is the fire of love that inspires the flute.
It is the ferment of love that completes the wine.
The reed is a comfort to all estranged lovers.
Its music tears our veils away. Have you
ever seen a poison or antidote like the reed?
It sings of the path of blood,
it relates the passion of Majnun.
Only to the senseless is this sense confided.
Does the tongue have any patron but the ear?
Our days grow more unseasonable in this pain,
these days which mix with grief . . .
but if our days are gone, say to them, "Go,
it doesn't matter," but You, You remain,
for nothing is as pure as You are.
All quickly fill with His water except the fish,

and the day is long without His daily bread.
The raw do not understand the state of the ripe,
and so my words shall be brief, good-bye!

Break your bonds, be free, my son!
How long will silver and gold enslave you?
If you pour the whole sea into a jug,
how much will it hold? One day's store.
The greedy eye, like the jug, is never filled.
Until content, the oyster holds no pearl.
Only one whose garment has been stripped by Love
has become free of defect and desire.
Oh Gladness, oh Love, our partner in trade,
healer of all our ills, our Plato and Galen,
remedy for our pride and vanity.
With love this earthly body could travel the air,
the mountain could get up and nimbly dance.
Love gave life to Mount Sinai, oh lover;
Sinai was drunk, Moses lost consciousness.
Pressed to the lips of one in harmony with myself,
I might also tell all that can be told,
but without a common tongue I am dumb
even if I have a hundred songs to sing.
When the rose is gone and the garden faded,
you will no longer hear the nightingale's song.
The Beloved is all, the lover just a veil.
The Beloved is living, the lover a dead thing.
If Love withholds its strengthening care,
the lover is left like a bird without wings.
How will I be awake and aware
if the light of the Beloved is absent?
Love wills that this Word be brought forth.
If you find the mirror of the heart dull,
the rust has not yet been cleared from its face.

Mathnawí, opening lines.

I darkened my eyes with the dust of sadness
until each of them was a sea full of pearls.
All the tears which we creatures shed for His sake
are not tears as many think, but pearls. . .
I am complaining about the Soul of the soul,
but I'm no complainer, I'm simply telling it.
My heart tells me it is distressed with Him,
but I can only laugh at such pretended injuries.
Do right, You who are the glory of the just.
You, Soul, who are liberated from "We" and "I,"
subtle spirit in man and woman,
when man and woman become one, that one is You,
and when that one is obliterated, there You are.
Where is this "We" and "I"? By the side of the Beloved.
You made this "We" and "I" in order that
you might play this game of service with Yourself,
that You and I might become one soul
and in the end to drown in the Beloved.
All this is true. Come! You *command of Being,*
You so far beyond description or naming.
Is it possible for the bodily eye to see You?
Can thought comprehend your laughter or grief?
Can the heart possessed by laughter or grief,
tell me now, can it possibly see You at all?
Such a heart has only these borrowed things to live with.
The garden of Love is green without limit
and yields many fruits other than sorrow or joy.
Love is beyond either condition:
without spring, without autumn, it is always fresh.

Mathnawí, I, 1779-1808.

What shall I do, O Muslims?
I do not recognize myself. . .
I am neither Christian nor Jew,
nor Magian, nor Muslim.
I am not of the East, nor the West,
not of the land, nor the sea.
I am not from nature's mine,
nor from the circling stars.
I am neither of earth nor water,
neither of wind nor fire.
I am not of the empyrean,
nor of the dust on this carpet.
I am not of the deep, nor from behind.
I am not of India nor China,
not of Bulgaria, nor Saqsin;
I am not of the kingdom of Iraqain,
nor of the land of Khorasan.
I am not of this world nor the next,
not of heaven, nor of purgatory.
My place is the placeless,
my trace is the traceless.
It is not the body nor is it the soul,
for I belong to the soul of my love.
I have put duality away
and seen the two worlds as one.
One I seek, One I know,
One I see, One I call.
*He is the first, He is the last.*
*He is the outward, He is the inward.*
I know of nothing but *Hu*, none but Him.
Intoxicated with the cup of Love,
two worlds slip from my hands.
I am occupied with nothing
but fun and carousing.

If once in my life I pass a moment without You,
I repent my life from that moment on.
If once in this world
I should win a moment with You,
I will put both worlds below my feet
and dance forever in joy.
Oh Shams of Tabríz, I am so drunk in the world
that except for revelry and intoxication
I have no tale to tell.

On that day when names did not exist,
nor any sign of anything to name, *I was*.
Things and their names came from me,
but that day was before "me" or "us".
A wisp of Love's hair was given as a sign
and yet that wisp of hair was not.
Cross and Christians end to end,
but Love was not yet upon the cross.
At the house of idols, at the ancient temple
not a trace was to be seen.
To the mountains I went: Herat and Kandahar,
and saw nothing, above or below.
I climbed to the summit of Mount Qaf
and found only the Simurgh there.
The reins of my search led to the Kaaba,
but Love was not at that goal of old and young.
I asked Ibn Sinna in his ecstasy,
but it was not within his extent.
I was "within two bow-lengths"
and found nothing in that high court.
I paid attention to my heart:
and that was the place, nowhere else.
Except for Shamsi Tabríz, that pure spirit,
no one ever was intoxicated, distraught, and in love.

This is love: to fly toward a secret sky,
to cause a hundred veils to fall each moment.
First to let go of life.
Finally, to take a step without feet.
To regard this world as invisible,
and to disregard what appears to the self.
Heart, I said, what a gift it has been
to enter this circle of lovers,
to see beyond seeing itself,
to reach and feel within the breast.
My soul, where does this breathing arise?
How does this beating heart exist?
Bird of the soul, speak in your own words
and I will understand.
The heart replied: I was in the work place
the day this house of water and clay was fired.
I was already flying from that created house
even while the house was being created.
When I could no longer resist, I was dragged down,
and my features were molded from a lump.

Oh Lord, said David, if you have no need for us,
then why did you create the two worlds?
Reality replied: Oh Temporal Man, I was a hidden treasure —
I wanted this treasure of kindness and generosity to be known
I produced a mirror — its face the heart, its back the world.
The back will please you if you've never seen the face.
Mixing mud and straw does not make a mirror,
yet by separating straw from mud, a mirror is revealed.
Until the juice ferments awhile in the cask, it isn't wine.
If you wish your heart to be bright, you must do a little work.
My King addressed the soul of my flesh:
You return the same as you left —
where are the traces of my gifts?
It is known that alchemy transforms copper to gold.
This Sun does not want a crown or robe from God's grace.
He is a hat to a hundred bald men, a cloak to ten naked.
Jesus sat on an ass in humility, my child!
How could a zephyr ride on the back of an ass?
Oh spirit, direct your search like the waters of a stream.
Oh reason, tread the path of selflessness into eternity.
Remember God so much that you are forgotten,
until you are lost in the Call,
without distinction of caller and called.

This house in which continual music is heard,
ask the landlord about this house.
Why these idol-like forms in this Kaaba?
Why the light of God in a Magian temple?
A treasure's in this house
which a world could not contain.
As for house and landlord,
it's all pretending and play.
Keep your hands off this house, this talisman.
Don't speak with the landlord,
he's drunk every night.
The dirt and garbage is all musk and scent.
The roof and door are verse and music.
In short, whoever finds his way to this house
is Sultan of the world, Solomon of his time.
Turn your head down, Lord, from the roof,
for I am hopeful of the luck in your good face.
I swear by your soul that after seeing your face
the whole earthly realm is fraud and fantasy.
The garden is bewildered as to which is leaf
and which is blossom. The distracted birds
can't distinguish the birdseed from the trap.
This is the Lord of Heaven, resembling venus and the moon.
This is the house of love, without limits or bounds.
Like a mirror the soul receives your image in the heart.
As if the curl of his hair penetrated their hearts like a comb,
within the presence of Joseph, women cut their wrists.
Come here, Soul, the beloved One is with us.
Everyone in this house is drunk; none know
whether so-and-so enters or so-and-so leaves.
Don't sit at the door intoxicated —
come quickly inside the house.
Whoever waits on the threshold remains in the dark.
Those drunk with God, though thousands, are one.

But drunk with lust even one is double.
Enter the wood of lions without fear of a wound.
Your thoughts and terrors are maidenly fancies.
For there is no wound: all is mercy and love.
But your thoughts are the bar behind the door.
Set fire to the wood. Silence, heart!
Hold your tongue, the tongue which is harmful.

*I* heard someone say: Master Sana'i is dead.
The death of such a master is no small thing.
He was not some straw pushed by the wind,
he was not water that froze in winter,
he was not a comb that broke in the hair,
he was not a seed which the earth swallowed.
He was a treasure of gold in this dustpit,
because he valued the whole world at a single barleycorn.
The earthly frame he tossed to earth.
Soul and intellect he raised aloft.
How curiously the elixir blends with the dregs,
until it settles out within the bottle.
A second soul which the mass of men never know,
I swear by God, he gave to his Beloved.
On a journey it often happens, my friend,
that the man of Merv or Rayy, the Roman and the Kurd
travel together before each returns home.
Should an old man be the companion of youths?
Be silent as a compass, the King
has erased your name from the book of speech.

That spirit which does not wear
the inner garment of Love
should never have been.
Its being is just shame.

Be drunken with Love,
for Love is all that exists.
Where is intimacy found,
if not in the give and take of Love?

If they ask what Love is,
say, the sacrifice of will.
If you have not left will behind,
you have no will at all.

The lover is a king of kings
with both worlds beneath him;
and a king does not regard
what lies at his feet.

Only Love and the lover
can resurrect beyond time.
Give your heart to this —
the rest is second-hand.

How long will you embrace
a lifeless beloved?
Embrace that entity
to which nothing can cling.

What sprouts up every spring
will wither by autumn,
but the rose-garden of Love
needs no special season.

Both the rose and the thorn
appear together in spring,
and the wine of the grape
is not without its headaches.

Do not be an impatient
bystander on this path —
by God there is no death
worse than expectancy.

Set your heart on hard cash
if you are not counterfeit,
and listen to my advice
if you are not a slave:

Don't falter on the horse
of the body — go lighter on foot.
God gives wings to those
who are not content to ride an ass.

Let go of your worries
and be completely clear hearted,
Like the face of a mirror
that contains no images.

When it is empty of forms,
all forms are contained in it.
No face would be ashamed
to be so clear.

If you want a clear mirror,
behold yourself,
and see the shameless truth
which the mirror reflects.

If metal can be polished
to a mirror-like finish —
what polishing does the mirror
of the heart require?

Between the mirror and the heart
is this single difference:
the heart conceals secrets
while the mirror does not.

*E*ach form you see has its unseen archetype,
if the form should pass, its essence is eternal.
If you have known beauty in a face or wisdom in a word,
let this counsel your heart: what perishes is not real.
Since the springhead is timeless, its branches refresh.
Since neither can cease, what is the cause of your sorrow?
Think of your soul as the source and created things as springs.
While the source exists, the springs continually flow.
Empty your head of grief and drink from the stream.
Don't think of it failing — this water is endless.
From the moment you came into the manifest world
a ladder was given that you might escape.
From mineral substance you were transformed to plant,
and later to animal. How could this be hidden?
Afterwards, as man, you developed knowledge, consciousness,
     faith.
See how this body has risen from the dust like a rose?
When you have walked on from man you will be an angel,
and done with this earth your place will be beyond.
Pass, then, from the angelic and enter the Sea.
Your drop will merge with a hundred Seas of Oman.
Leave him you called "Son," and say "One" with your life.
Although your body has aged, your soul has become young.

*M*erge yourself with the community and know the joy of the soul
Enter the streets of ruin with those who drink to the dregs.
Empty the glass of your desire so that you are not disgraced.
Close both the eyes in your head and find the inner eye.
Open your arms if you want an embrace.
Break the idol of clay and behold the radiance!
Why get tied to a hag like this world, and for such a price?
And for a ration of three loaves why think of the sword and knife?
At night the Beloved always returns, take no opium tonight.
Close your mouth to food and know another taste.
The cup-bearer is no tyrant — his gathering is a circle.
Come into the circle, sit down beyond the turning of time.
Here is the bargain: give one life and receive a hundred.
Stop behaving like dogs and experience the shepherd's care.
You complain of someone who took what you had?
Well, forget him for the presence of Him.
Think of nothing but the source of thought.
Care of the soul is more than your hunger for bread.
Why in this wide world do you sleep in a prison?
Avoid complicated thinking; the explanation is in higher worlds.
Limit your talk for the sake of eternal communication.
Abandon life and the world, and find the life of the world.

The man of God is drunken while sober.
The man of God is full without meat.
The man of God is perplexed and bewildered.
The man of God neither sleeps nor eats.
The man of God is a king clothed in rags.
The man of God is a treasure in the streets.
The man of God is neither of sky nor land.
The man of God is neither of fire nor sea.
The man of God is an ocean without end.
The man of God drops pearls at your feet.
The man of God has a hundred moons at night.
The man of God has a hundred suns' light.
The man of God's knowledge is complete.
The man of God doesn't read with his sight.
The man of God is beyond form and disbelief.
The man of God sees good and bad alike.
The man of God is far beyond non-being.
The man of God is seen riding high.
The man of God is hidden, Shamsuddin.
The man of God you must seek and find.

With every breath the sound
of love surrounds us,
and we are bound for the depths
of space, without sightseeing.
We've been in orbit before
and know the angels there.
Let's go there again, Master,
for that is our land.
Yet we are beyond all that
and something more than angels.
Out beyond duality,
we have a home, and it is Glory.
That pure substance is
different from this dusty world.
What kind of place is this?
We once came down, soon we'll return.
A new happiness befriends us
as we work at offering our lives.
Muhammed, an ornament to the world,
is our caravan's chosen guide.
The sweetness we breathe on the wind
is from the scent of his hair,
and the radiance of this thought
is from the light of his day.
His face once split the moon in two —
she couldn't endure the sight of him.
Yet how lucky she was,
she who humbly received him.
Look into our hearts and see
the splitting moon in each breath.
Having seen that vision,
how can you still dream?
When the wave of *Am I not?* struck,
it wrecked the body's ship;

when the ship wrecks once more,
it will be the time of union.
Man, like a bird of the sea,
emerged from the ocean of the soul.
Earth is not the final rest
of a bird born of that sea.
No, we are pearls of that ocean,
all of us live in it;
and if it weren't so, why would
wave upon wave arrive?
This is the time of union,
the time of eternal beauty.
It is the time of luck and kindness,
it is the ocean of purity.
The wave of Bestowal has come.
The roar of the sea is here.
The morning of happiness has dawned,
no — it is the light of God.
Whose face is pictured here?
Who is this shah or prince?
Who is this aged intelligence?
They are all masks . . .
and the only remedy is
this boiling ecstasy of the soul.
A fountain of refreshment
is in the head and eyes,
not the earthly head of clay,
but another pure, heavenly one.
But many a pure head has been spilled
beneath the dust. Know one from the other!
The original head is hidden,
while the other head is visible.
Beyond this world is a world
that has no boundaries.

Tie up the water skin, brother,
and draw some wine from our cask!
The clay jug of perception
has such a narrow spout.
From Tabríz the sun appeared,
and I said,
this light is at once joined
with all things, and yet apart from all.

*A*t the break of dawn a single moon appeared,
descended from the sky, and gazed at me.
Like a falcon swooping in for the catch
it snatched me up and soared across the sky.
When I looked at myself, I saw myself no more,
because by grace my body had become fine.
I made a journey of the soul accompanied by the moon,
until the secret of time was totally revealed.
Heaven's nine spheres were in that moon.
The vessel of my being had vanished in the sea.
Waves rose on the ocean. Intelligence ascended
and sounded its call. So it happened, so it was.
The sea began to foam and every bit of froth
took shape and was bodied forth.
Each spindrift body which received a sign from that sea
immediately melted and became spirit in that ocean.
Without the power of Shams 'l Haqq of Tabriz
one could neither behold the moon nor become the sea.

*O*h lovers, lovers, it is time
  to set out from the world.
The drum of celestial distances
sounds in my soul's ear.
The camel driver is at work
and has prepared the caravan.
He asks that we forgive him
for the disturbance he has caused us,
but why are we travelers asleep?
Everywhere the murmur of departure,
and the stars, like candles
thrust at us from behind blue veils,
and as if to make the invisible more plain,
a wondrous people have come forth.

Beneath this water-wheel of stars
your sleep has been heavy.
Observe that heaviness and beware. . .
for life is fragile and quick.
Heart, aim yourself at Love!
Friend, discover the Friend!
Watchman, wake-up!
You weren't put here to sleep!
Noise and alarm on every side,
candles and torches, tonight
this pregnant world gives birth to eternity.
Lifeless clay is living heart.
The inept become aware.
What draws you now
will lead you further,
and as it draws you to itself,
what pleasure your suffering becomes.
Its fires are like water,
do not tense your face.
To be present in the soul is its work,

and to break your vows.
By its complex art these atoms
are trembling in their hearts.

Oh vain puppet, proclaiming
your importance from a hole,
how long will you leap?
Humble yourself, or they will break you!
You have tended seeds of deceit
and practiced contempt.
Oh pimp, the eternal truth
was cheapened in your hands!
Oh ass, you deserve only straw,
and were better black like a pot.

There is another within me
by whom these eyes sparkle.
If water scalds it is by fire,
let this be understood.
I have no stone in my hand,
no quarrel with anyone.
I rebuke no man, but possess
the sweetness of the rose-garden.
My eye is from that source
and from another universe.
One world on this side, another on that,
as I sit on the threshold.
On the threshold are they alone
whose language is silence.
Enough has been uttered,
say no more, hold back the tongue.

Shouldn't the soul arise
when a gentle prompting
from the source of all strength
calls it to flight?
Shouldn't a fish, when it hears
the sound of waves, flip
from the shore into the sea?
Wouldn't the falcon on hearing
the drum beating "Return, return!"
leave the hunt and rejoin the King?
Shouldn't every sufi dance
like a speck in the eternal sun
and save himself from decay?
Such grace and beauty, such giving
of life that to ignore it
could only bring pain and misfortune.
Return then, fly home,
your feathered wings outspread,
for you have escaped the cage!
Abandon your stagnant pool
for the running waters of life.
Come out of the vestibule
to the soul's place of honor.
Go ahead, for we are coming too,
from the world of separation
to the world of union.
How long will we fill our pockets
with dirt and stones like children?
Let us release this earth and rise.
Let us leave childish things behind
and sit at the table of men.
See how this earthly frame
has trapped you? Let's split the sack
and stick our necks out!

Take this letter of love
in your right hand. You're not a child,
remember your left from your right!
God said to Reason's herald, "Begone!"
To the hand of Death he said:
"Anoint only the ear of lust."
A call came to the soul:
Go to the unseen world.
Take the gain and the goods
and lament the pain no more.
Cry out and claim your kingship.
The gift of an answer will be yours;
and the knowledge behind the question.

Inside my Self I discover
the scent of the Friend in every breath.
Why not hold this Self close every night?

Last night in Love's garden
an urge ran through my head;
His sun shined from my eyes;
spirit, like a river, began to flow.

Each laughing rose
that springs from His lips
has avoided the thorn of existence,
has escaped the sword of corruption.

Every tree and plant in the meadow
seemed to be dancing,
those which average eyes
would see as fixed and still.

Suddenly our tall Cypress appeared.
The garden lost itself entirely,
and the plane tree clapped its hands.

A face like fire, wine like fire,
love afire — all three happy together.
From the blending of these fires
the soul was wailing, "Let me out of here!"

In the world of unity
there's no room for number.
But out of necessity number exists
in the worlds of five and four.

Count a hundred thousand
sweet apples in your hands;

if you wish to make one,
crush them all together!

Without considering the letters,
listen to the language of the heart.
Purity of color is a quality
derived from the source of action.

The Sun of Tabríz is on the throne,
while my verses line up like willing slaves.

For the sake of God, the Real,
whose slave I am, I wield this sword.
The body does not command me,
nor does the lion of craving
overcome the lion of God.
Like a sword wielded by the sun,
I manifest these words in war:
*Thou didst not throw when thou threwest.*
I have dropped the baggage of self.
That which is not God is nothing.
God is the sun and I am a shadow.
Jeweled with the pearls of Union,
my sword brings life in battle, not death.
Blood will not dull my shining sword,
nor will the wind sweep my sky away.
I am not chaff, but a mountain of patience.
What fierce wind could lift a mountain?
What the wind blows away is trash,
and winds blow from every side.
The winds of anger, lust, and greed
carried off him who did not keep
the times of prayer. I am a mountain
and my being is His building.
If I am tossed like a straw,
it is His wind that moves me.
Only His wind stirs my desires.
My Captain is Love of the One.
Anger is a king over kings,
but anger, once bridled, may serve.
A gentle sword struck the neck of anger.
God's anger came on like mercy.
My roof in ruins, I drown in light.

Though called "the father of dust"
I have grown like a garden.
And so I must put down my sword,
that my name might be *He loves for God's sake,*
that my desire may be *He hates for God's sake,*
that my generosity may be *He gives for God's sake,*
that my being may be *He witholds for God's sake.*
My stinginess is for God, as are my gifts.
I belong to God, not to anyone else;
and what I do is not a show,
not imagined, not thought up, but seen.
Set free from effort and searching,
I have tied my sleeve to the hem of God—
if I am flying, I see where I fly,
if I am circling, I know the axis on which I turn,
if I am dragging a burden, I know to where.
I am the moon and the sun is before me.
I cannot tell the people more than this—
can the river contain the Sea?

*Mathnawi,* I, 3787-3810

On that fatal day when my casket rolls along
do not think my heart is in this world.
Do not cry, do not cry with anguished moans,
for that is a pit a demon has dug, and only that is sad.
When you see my procession, don't cry, "Gone, gone!"
For me it is a time of meeting and reunion.
As you lower me into the grave, don't say, "So long."
The grave is a veil before the gathering of paradise.
When you see that lowering down, consider a rising.
What harm is there in the setting of a sun or moon?
What seems a setting to you is a dawning.
Though it may seem a prison,
this vault releases the soul.
What seed goes into the earth and does not grow?
Why are you doubting this human seed?
What bucket goes down and does not come up full?
Why should the Joseph of the spirit resent the well?
Shut your mouth on this side and open it beyond,
for in the nowhere air will be your song.

Word has just come:
    perhaps you haven't heard?
The envious heart is bleeding!
Perhaps you have no heart?
The moon revealed its face
and opened its wings of light.
Borrow the eyes and heart
of someone else if you must.

Day and night an arrow flies
from a hidden bow. What can you do?
Yield up your sweet life,
you have no shield.
Like Moses the copper of your being
has turned to gold by this alchemy.
So what if your sack
isn't filled with the gold of Korah?

An Egypt is within you,
you are its fields of sugar cane,
yet appearances enslave you –
you're occupied with idols.
You resemble Joseph, yet cannot glimpse
your own beauty. By God,
when you see it in the mirror,
you will be the idol of yourself.

Oh Reason, aren't you unjust
to compare him to the moon?
How can you say that?
Perhaps you have no eyes
to see his face. Your head
is a lamp with six wicks.
How will all six be lit
if you have no spark?

Your body is a camel
that travels to the Kaaba of the heart.
You were asinine not to go,
it's not that you have no ass.
If you have not gone to the Kaaba,
destiny will draw you there.
Don't run off babbling —
there is no escape from God.

*A*t the last you vanished, gone to the unseen.
　　Strange, strange, the path you took out of this world.
The power of your beating wings demolished the cage,
you took to the air, and went for the world of the soul.

You were a favorite falcon in the hands of an old woman,
but when you heard the falcon-drum, you flew to the placeless.
You were a drunken nightingale among owls,
but when the fragrance of the rose-garden reached you,
you were gone to that rose-garden.

The bitter wine you consumed here with us left you head-sore,
but at last you entered the eternal tavern.
Like an arrow you went straight for the mark of bliss,
straight to the mark like an arrow from this bow.

Like a ghoul the world deceived you with false clues,
but you refused the clues and went straight for that which had
　　　　no clue.
Since you are now the sun, what will you do with your crown?
and how will you fasten your belt now that you've vanished
　　　　from the middle?

Oh heart, what a rare bird you are, that in your search
　　　　for heavenly attention,
you flew on two wings to the spear-point like a shield!
The rose flees from autumn, but what a foolhardy rose you are,
lingering behind in the presence of the autumn wind.

You were the rain of another world falling on our dusty earth.
You ran in every direction until you escaped down the gutter.
Be silent and be free of the pain of speech. Do not sleep,
since you have found refuge with so loving a friend.

APPENDIX: *A Note on the Thirteenth Century.*

Jeláluddín Rúmí was born in 1207 in the city of Balkh in the Persian province of Khorasan, in what is present day Afghanistan. He was from a distinguished family which traced itself back to Abú Bakr, the first caliph of Islam. His father, Bahá'uddín, was a professor of religion, one of the most eminent in that great city. Despite their comfortable situation, Bahá'uddín decided to uproot his family and seek a new home somewhere to the south, for these were the days of Chengiz Khan, when much of central Asia and the world was being overrun by the Mongol hordes. The step was well taken, because Balkh would eventually be sacked and most of its inhabitants slaughtered.

The family first traveled to Níshápúr where they were met by the great poet Faríduddín Attar, who presented the young Jelál with a copy of his *Asrár-náma (Book of Mysteries)* and said: "This child is destined to set the hearts of many aflame." The family would travel to Baghdad, Mecca, and Damascus, before finally settling in Konya (Iconium), capital of the Seljuk Empire, a stable and peaceful haven in those times. In Konya Bahá'uddín accepted an important teaching position, which his son would inherit, and this ancient city on the high Anatolian plain would become the lifelong home of Jelál and his descendants for generations to come.

The thirteenth century was a time of fruition and destruction, of decadence and rebirth. Peter of Aragon had approved the burning of heretics in 1197, and Pope Innocent III staged a twenty year campaign of extermination against the Cathari (1209-1229), a heretical sect that emphasized poverty and simplicity. Whole cities were slaughtered if even half the population was suspected of being associated with the sect. It was around this time that Pope Innocent IV sanctioned the torture of heretics and the distribution of their property among lay officials.

While the Inquisition was beginning in Europe, and Chengiz Khan was ravaging much of the Eastern lands, many of the greatest spiritual personalities of the last two thousand years were planting seeds that would be harvested for centuries to come. The twelfth century had seen the establishment of scholasticism in Europe with Paris and Oxford becoming famed for theology. It was at this time that Albertus Magnus brought so much through his Arabian commentaries, and his student, Thomas Aquinas (1225-1274), would be responsible for introducing many Neoplatonist ideas into Christianity. Saint Dominic founded an order based on apostolic poverty in 1216, and Saint Francis is known to have been preaching before the Sultan of Egypt in 1219. Meister Eckhart and Johannes Tauler, both Dominicans, were developing a Celtic-Germanic mysticism that had much in common with the metaphysics of Spain's Ibn 'Arabí, who was nearly their contemporary.

This same period produced most of the names associated with the greatest literary and spiritual achievements of Islam since the days of the Prophet and his companions. Late in the twelfth century Al Ghazzálí had succeeded in integrating the mystical ideas of Sufism with orthodox theology, and thereby bringing these ideas more into the mainstream. In Persia, Suhrawardí Maqtúl (1153-1191) had synthesized a grand theosophy of illumination from Islamic and ancient Persian sources, incorporating the wisdom of centuries if not millennia. In this century, too, Sana'i wrote *Hadíqat al-haqíqa* (The Orchard of Truth), which became the model for much of the didactic mystical poetry that followed, including Rumí's *Mathnáwi*.

The heights of Islamic metaphysical speculation were

reached by Ibn 'Arabí (1165-1240), known as "the Pole of Knowledge." It was he who wrote: "God becomes the mirror in which the spiritual man contemplates his own reality and in turn becomes the mirror in which God contemplates His names and qualities." Sadruddín Qónawí (d.1274), his disciple and foremost interpreter, emigrated to Konya and was closely associated with Mevlána.

In addition to Attár, already mentioned, Ibn al-Faríd (d.1235), another great poet of mystical love, wrote his delicate and refined verses in Egypt. While in Turkey, Yunus Emre sang his songs of mystical love in the Turkish vernacular. Another immigrant from Khorasán at this time was the great and enigmatic Hadji Bektash (1247-1338), founder of an important dervish order. Meanwhile, Muiniddín Chistí arrived in Delhi just fourteen years before Mevlána's birth. He and his successors were responsible for the introduction of Islam into India through a lively and devotional Sufism that gained great popularity among the people. In briefest outline these are some of the personalities that helped to make the thirteenth century an unrivaled time for mystical inspiration.